QUINTES

Quilting

HB
HINKLER
BOOKS

Creative director: Sam Grimmer
Designer: Rebecca Buttrose
Prepress: Splitting Image

First published in 2007
by Hinkler Books Pty Ltd
45–55 Fairchild Street
Heatherton Victoria 3202 Australia
www.hinklerbooks.com

© Universal Magazines 2007
www. universalmagazines.com.au

4 6 8 10 9 7 5 3
08 10 09

Printed and bound in China

HB
HINKLER
BOOKS

ISBN 978 1 7418 1332 6

CONTENTS

Introduction

Welcome to *Quintessential Quilting*. This book is a practical, step-by-step guide for established quilters, or for those familiar with sewing, who are ready to create their first quilt.

Quintessential Quilting offers useful information for quilting beginners, as well as advice for more experienced quiltmakers. *Quintessential Quilting* will acquaint you with the tools, techniques and stitches needed on your quilting adventures. The programs will provide you with the information necessary to create five magnificent quilts.

The detailed full-colour programs included in this set are step-by-step guides, incorporating easy-to-follow diagrams, templates and helpful hints. The pieces in this book range from easy-to-make to challenging quilts.

Quintessential Quilting will provide you with a range of quilting possibilities, providing inspiration and guidance in your quilting endeavours.

A quilter's companion

Before you embark on any quilting project, and especially if this is your first quilt, you'll need to make sure you have all the equipment and information necessary for a successful project. Many of the items required are normal sewing supplies and any special tools can be found in your local quilt shop.

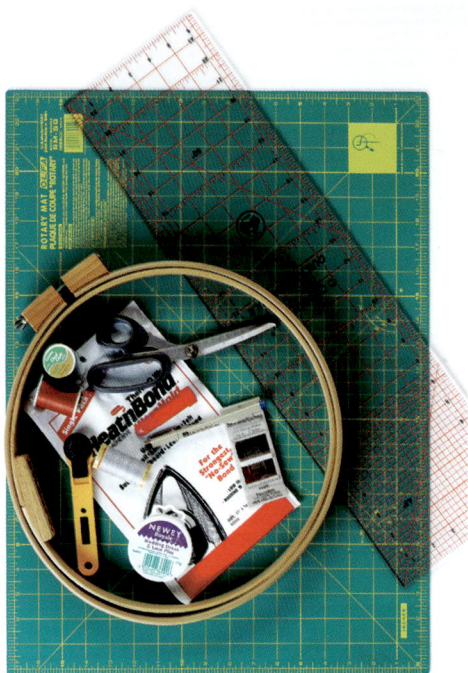

Tools of the trade

If you enjoy sewing by hand, it's quite feasible to start your first quilt project with little more than thread, pins, needles, scissors, iron and fabric. Machinists need only add a basic sewing machine – no fancy stitches required. Over time, you may add to your tool kit as your interests and knowledge develop. Our basic list looks like this:

Sewing machine Any machine can be used for quiltmaking. It is helpful to have a darning foot as an attachment for the machine for free machine quilting.

Iron and ironing board Make these readily available near your sewing machine so that all seams can be pressed to assist in accurate piecing.

Needles Most quilters favour a 'between' needle, size 8–12 for both hand sewing and hand quilting. Size 12, the smallest size, is usually used by very experienced quilters.

Sewing thread Use any cotton or cotton-covered polyester thread. For machine quilting, use cotton, cotton-covered polyester, monofilament or decorative threads.

Scissors Have one pair with sharp points for cutting fabric and a second pair for paper.

Marking tools Quilters use marking tools for many varied processes during quiltmaking. Keep hard and soft lead pencils and fine-tipped permanent marking pens on hand. There are many specialist marking tools for quilters on the market, including chalk pencils and water-erasable markers, and it is best to experiment with several different types to see which suits you best. It is most important to test every marker before using it.

Rotary cutter and mat These tools quickly and accurately cut strips, squares, triangles and diamonds for patchwork. Always use your rotary cutter with a mat.

Quilter's ruler This acrylic ruler is used with the rotary cutter and allows you to cut perfectly straight lines. There are many sizes available and it is a good idea to gradually build up a collection. To begin with, choose a 14in x 4.5in ruler with ¼in divisions and 45 and 60 degree angles and a 6.5in square ruler again with ¼in divisions.

Template plastic This is used for making templates. The frosted side of the transparent plastic can be drawn on with pencil.

Quilting hoop These have a greater diameter and are deeper than an embroidery hoop to cope with the thickness of the quilt. The quilt is stretched in the hoop when hand quilting.

Quilting thread A 100% cotton thread that is stronger than normal sewing thread and is used when quilting by hand.

Thimble Use a thimble to protect your finger when pushing the needle through the three layers of the quilt.

Safety Pins Have several hundred 1in or 1.5in nickel plated safety pins available for pinning the three layers of the quilt together prior to quilting.

Fabric

People come to quiltmaking from many different directions. Some have had a lifelong love of textiles and may already have acquired a large stash of fabrics. For others, quiltmaking is their first sewing experience since school days: they don't even have a needle or pin in the house, let alone a hoard of cotton fabrics!

Type of fabric

Most quiltmakers recommend 100% high-quality cotton fabric, which can be purchased from small specialty shops as well as large chains. Cotton fabrics have a number of characteristics not shared by man-made fibres or other natural products, which make them ideal for quiltmaking. Cotton retains a crease, making a clean edge for appliqué and a neat finish to a patchwork seam. Cotton is easy to sew because of its softness. It tears on the grain, which is particularly important in fabric lengths used for borders, and it is usually more opaque than polyester fabrics, reducing the problem of seams being visible through the quilt top.

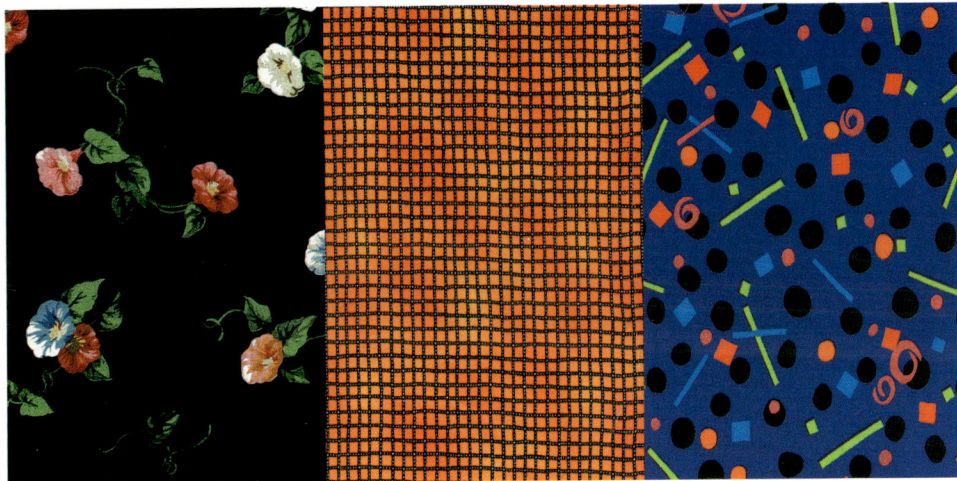

Choosing fabrics

Many quiltmakers struggle with the choice of fabrics for their quilt. The best advice is to trust yourself and use colours that you love.

If your project is based on a quilt that you've seen in a magazine or book, study the design carefully to understand why it works and what appeals to you. Look particularly to see how the different value of various fabrics (light, medium, dark), the different style of prints (geometric, floral, checks, pictorial, tone-on-tone, solids etc) and the scale of the prints (small, medium, large) contribute to the overall effect. Visit quilt shows, observing the colours and effects that appeal to you as well as those that don't. Search for quilts on the Internet.

To help build confidence, buy small amounts of fabric and make some practice blocks or pieces to see how your choices work together. This will enable you to experiment without spending a lot of money.

Preparing to use your fabric

Wash any fabric before using it in your quilt. This way, the fabric pre-shrinks, loose dye bleeds from the fabric and finishes that increase stiffness are washed out.

If you choose to pre-wash your fabrics, use either no detergent at all, or a very mild one. Some detergents made especially for quilts are available in specialist shops. Wash your fabrics in a washing machine in warm water on a gentle cycle.

There are, however, many quiltmakers who prefer to work with unwashed fabrics. They like the crispness of the fabric straight off the bolt, or they like the 'instant antique' look that is achieved when the finished quilt is washed, then dried in a dryer. The fabric shrinkage that occurs causes slight puckers along the quilting lines, which is reminiscent of old quilts. If you choose not to pre-wash your fabrics, it is still advisable to test for colourfastness prior to use. Hand wash a small swatch of the fabric and allow it to dry on a white paper towel, looking for any colour transfer.

Rotary cutting

Before cutting any fabric for your project, press it well to eliminate any wrinkles or creases. Do all rotary cutting on a self-healing mat and at a height that is comfortable for you to work at while standing – a kitchen bench is often best. To cut strips the width of the fabric, fold the fabric wrong sides together so that the selvedges match up. The fabric is now about 21in wide. Place the fabric on the mat with the fold closest to you. If you are right handed, start working from the right-most raw edge. If you are left handed, start working from the left-most raw edge. Create a straight edge by aligning one of the horizontal lines on your ruler exactly with the fold in the fabric. Trim the raw edge.

Turn the mat and the fabric together in a 180⁰ arc. To cut strips, position the ruler on top of the fabric, measuring in the required strip width from the newly cut edge. For example, for a 2in strip, align the raw edge of the fabric with the 2in mark on your ruler. Align one of the horizontal lines on the ruler exactly with the fold in the fabric again. Cut the length of the fabric, stopping when necessary to reposition your hand on the ruler to ensure that it doesn't move as you cut.

For rotary cutting, trim the raw edge first

Cutting 2in wide strips

If you have difficulty cutting strips across the 21in of fabric, experiment with folding the fabric again, so that it is four thickness and only 10 or 11 inches wide. Be extra careful when making the second fold – ensure that the first fold is exactly aligned with the selvedges. If it isn't, you will find that the strips you cut have bends in them. Check each strip as it is cut.

Once you've cut strips, it's easy to use your rotary cutter to make shapes that are commonly used in patchwork, such as squares, rectangles and triangles. To cut 2in squares, for example, you would begin by cutting a 2in strip. Unfold the strip, and align a horizontal line on the ruler with the top

edge and close to the selvedge. Remove the selvedge with a vertical cut. Turn the strip around 180^0, align the raw edge of the strip with the 2in vertical line on your rule and cut. You now have a 2in square. Continue cutting along the strip every 2in until you have as many squares as you need.

As your skills and confidence grow, you may prefer to cut your squares while the fabric strip is still folded. You will be cutting through two layers of fabric and creating two squares with each cut.

Rectangles are cut in the same manner except that the length of your shape will be different from the width of your strip. From a 2in strip, for example, you could cut rectangles that are 1in x 2in, 3in x 2in, 10in x 2in, and so on.

Cutting 2in squares easily from a 2in strip of fabric

Cross cutting

The instructions provided in many quilting projects tell you to start by cutting squares, and then 'cross cutting' the squares into triangles. To do this, follow the instructions on the previous page to create squares of the size required. Half-square triangles are made by cutting a square in half diagonally. Align the ruler so that its edge runs through two diagonally opposite corners of the fabric square, then cut along that edge.

Quarter-square triangles are made by cutting a square twice diagonally. Follow the instructions for making half-square triangles. After your first diagonal cut, lift the ruler carefully so that neither of the newly created triangles moves. Rotate the cutting board 90° and carefully place the edge of the ruler so that it runs through the other two diagonally opposite corners of the fabric square. Cut, being careful not to allow the fabric to shift.

Cutting half-square triangles

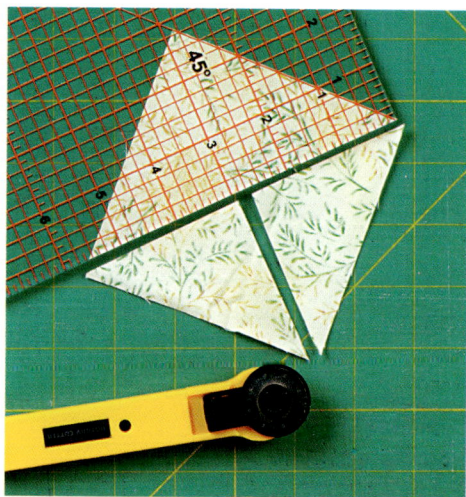

Cutting quarter-square triangles

Sewing by hand or machine?

Most quilt projects can be successfully completed by either hand or machine, or even a mixture of both. You might choose to sew by hand if:

- you don't own or have ready access to a sewing machine

- you expect to do your sewing when in the company of friends and family, and you would like to participate in their conversation

- you would like to do some sewing when you're away from home

- you find the process relaxing

- you don't enjoy using a sewing machine.

You might choose to sew by machine if:

- you have a machine

- you find using the machine simple and fun

- you prefer the faster speed with which your project comes together when using a machine

- you have a place where you can set up your machine permanently or get it set up fairly quickly

- you need to finish your project this week.

Accuracy

Quiltmaking is a joyful pastime. It can be fun, challenging, creative, satisfying, soothing and rewarding. Each quiltmaker needs to find their own level of workmanship. For most, of course, it will improve with experience and practice. But from the beginning, it is important to strive for accuracy in measuring, marking, cutting and sewing. A few millimetres here, an eighth of an inch there will add up and create difficulties when trying to assemble the quilt.

If sewing by hand, check every few stitches that you are sewing on the line marked on both patches. If sewing by machine, test that you are sewing a scant ¼in (or 7.5mm) seam and consider creating a guide on your machine with masking tape so that your seams are consistently accurate.

Making templates

Some people prefer to use templates for their patchwork. Even those who typically use template-free methods may find that it's easier to make a template for some unusual shapes.

A template is a durable pattern piece that can be used to cut out fabric. Templates are made by tracing the patterns provided in your project instructions onto stiff cardboard or purpose-made plastic, which can be purchased from specialty stores. If you're going to cut fabric and sew by hand, do not include seam allowances in your templates – they are added when cutting the fabric. If you are going to cut fabric with a rotary cutter or sew by machine, include seam allowances in your templates.

Mark the face of each template you make with the name of the project, its designated name or number, the grain line and whether or not seam allowances are included.

Using templates

To cut fabric by hand, use a well-sharpened yellow, silver or lead pencil to trace around the template shape. Place the template face down on the wrong side of the fabric. These lines are your sewing lines.

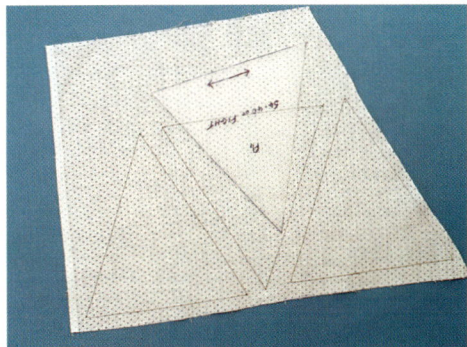

Using a carefully labeled template

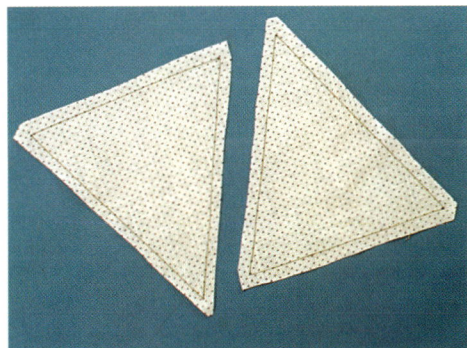

Cut-out fabric pieces

Position the outlines at least ½in (15mm) apart. As you cut out each fabric shape, add a seam allowance of about ¼in (7.5mm) – that is, don't cut on the marked line, but about ¼in (7.5mm) outside it.

To cut with a rotary cutter, start with a strip or a piece of fabric with a straight edge. Align a straight edge of your template with the straight edge of the fabric. Make sure that the grain line marked on each template is aligned with the grain of the fabric. Where practicable, position the edge of any pattern piece that will be on the outside edge of a patchwork block on the lengthwise grain of the fabric to minimise stretch.

Cutting out shapes using templates and a rotary cutter and ruler

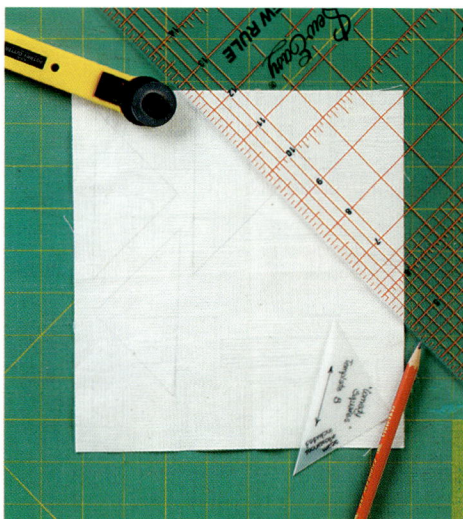

Using templates with seam allowance

Place your ruler against another edge of the template, remove the template and cut down the side of the ruler. Continue to do this until you have completed cutting out the shape.

Alternatively, you could trace around the template on the back of your fabric, align the edge of your ruler with one of the marked lines and cut. Remember that if you are going to cut this way you need to include seam allowances in your templates.

Hand piecing

Pin two pieces right sides together. Place pins perpendicular to the sewing line, making sure that there is a pin at the beginning and end points. Choose thread that matches the darkest fabric that you are sewing.

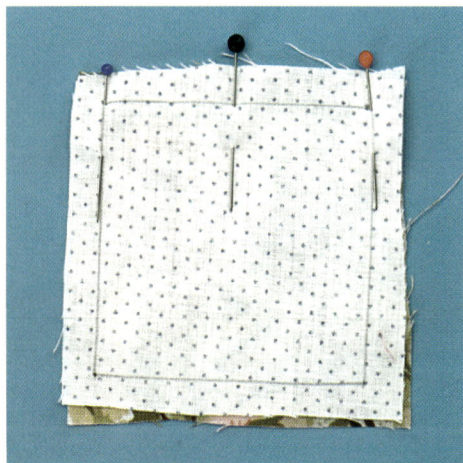

Pinning the pieces

Pinning the pieces

Tie a small knot in the end of the thread and insert the needle at the beginning of the marked sewing line. Sew along the line using a small running stitch – the smaller the better. Every now and then sew a backstitch. At the end of the marked line, sew a backstitch and a loop knot to finish. Do not sew across the seam allowances. When crossing seam intersections, backstitch just before the intersection, slip the needle through both fabrics to the other side and backstitch again. Then continue sewing as before.

Sewing through a join

Machine piecing

Machine piecing is typically done with a stitch length of 12–14 stitches per inch (2–2.5 stitch setting on some machines).

Pin two pieces right sides together. Place pins perpendicular to the sewing line, making sure there is a pin at the beginning and end points. Choose thread that matches the darkest fabric that you are sewing.

Place the pinned patches under the presser foot with the bulk of the fabric to the left and positioned so that you will sew a scant ¼in (or 7.5mm) seam. Begin stitching at the raw edge. There is no need to begin each seam with a backstitch. While some people prefer to sew over the pins, there is a risk that doing so will ruin the pin, break a needle or interfere with the timing of the machine, ultimately leading to expensive repairs.

You can set up an 'assembly line' by pinning a number of pairs of patches together and then sewing them one after another, without cutting the thread between them. When the line of chained pieces is completed, clip them apart.

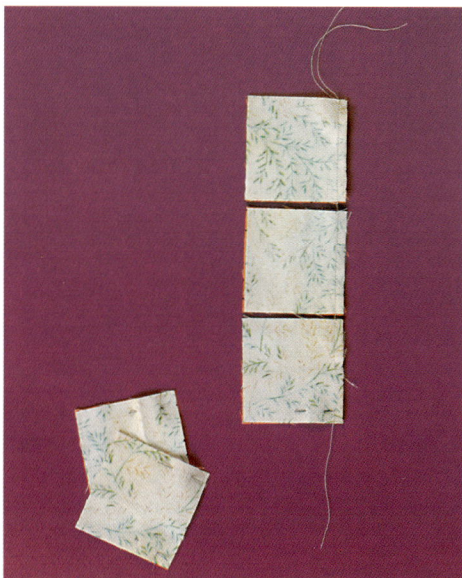

Chain piecing

Pressing

Pressing your patchwork is important. Use a dry iron when pressing seams as steam can stretch the fabric and distort it. Press by lifting and placing the iron on the fabric repeatedly – do not iron the patches by moving the iron back and forth over them.

Traditionally, seam allowances are pressed to one side – toward the darker fabric. Put the patches you have sewn together on the ironing board with the darker fabric on top and the seam allowance furthest away from you. Press the seam by placing the iron directly onto the line of stitching. Then lift the raw edge of the darker fabric, open out the patches and press the seam flat.

Pressing the seam flat

Appliqué

There are a number of appliqué methods, each requiring different preparation and tools. Whole books have been written on this topic! There is no one 'right' way, so experiment with a variety of methods to determine which one you find most comfortable. Three hand-appliqué techniques are included here; needleturn, freezer paper, and fusible web/ buttonhole.

Needleturn appliqué

For this method, appliqué templates are made in the same manner as for patchwork by hand (see 'Making templates' and 'Using templates' on page 14 and 15). The appliqué shape is cut out of fabric about ¼in outside the line traced around the template.

Pin or baste the appliqué shape to the background fabric. Choose thread to match the colour of the appliqué fabric, cut an 18in length and make a small knot in one end. Place the tip of the needle underneath the appliqué shape in the middle of one side. Bring the needle up through the fabric just inside the marked line and pull the thread through so that the knot is hidden underneath.

Hold the background fabric and appliqué shape with one hand, and with the other, use the tip of the needle to gently guide the edge of the appliqué fabric under so that the marked line is just out of sight. Press this fold with your thumb to form a crease, creating a neat edge for stitching. Insert the tip of the needle into the background fabric close to the crease. Bring it up again through the edge of the appliqué. Continue turning, creasing and stitching in this manner.

Needleturn appliqué – turning, creasing

Freezer-paper appliqué

Freezer paper is an American product. It is a plastic-coated paper originally designed for wrapping meat that was to be stored in a deep freezer. This product is now commonly available in specialty quilting shops. The paper used to wrap photocopying paper can also be used for this method of appliqué.

One widely used method for using freezer paper for appliqué is to place the freezer paper shiny (coated) side down over the appliqué pattern. Use a sharp pencil to trace the appliqué onto the paper, then cut out the shape on the traced line. This becomes your template.

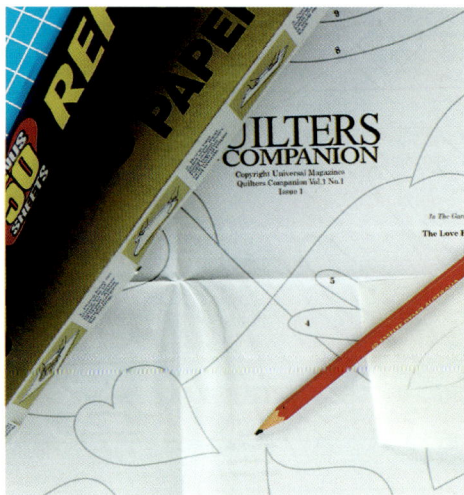

Trace the shape onto the paper side of the freezer paper

Place the shiny side of the paper on the wrong side of the fabric and press it in place using a hot dry iron. Cut out the appliqué fabric about ¼in (7.5mm) outside the edge of the paper. Turn the seam allowance over the edge of the paper and baste in place. Press.

Pin the shape to the background fabric. Stitch in place using a small blind stitch, which should pass through the edge of the fabric but not through the freezer paper template. To remove the freezer paper, you can either stop stitching about ¾in from your starting point, remove the basting, pull the freezer paper through the opening with tweezers and then complete the stitching; or you can completely stitch around the shape. To remove the basting, make a small cut in the background fabric behind the appliqué shape, and use tweezers to remove the freezer paper from behind.

Cutting out the appliqué shape

Removing the freezer paper from behind

Fusible web/buttonhole appliqué

Unlike the needleturn and freezer paper techniques described above, where the goal is to use small, virtually invisible appliqué stitching, buttonhole appliqué makes a feature of the stitching.

For this technique you will need to purchase double-sided fusible web, which is sold in specialty stores. Place the web with the paper-side up over the appliqué pattern. Use a sharp pencil to trace the appliqué on to the web, then cut out the shape roughly at least ¼in outside the traced line.

Place the web paper-side up on the wrong side of the fabric and press it in place following the manufacturer's guidelines. Cut out the appliqué fabric on the traced line. Peel the backing off the web and position the shape on the background fabric. Press it in place following the manufacturer's guidelines.

Stitch the appliqué in place using embroidery floss, size 8 pearl thread, or quilting thread. The thread colour could match the appliqué or, to make a real feature of the stitching, might contrast with it. Black thread has been used in days gone by.

Buttonhole stitching the shape

Cut a length of thread about 18in long, and tie a small knot in one end. Insert the needle from the back of the work so that it comes out through the background fabric only, just at the edge of the appliqué shape. Make a small buttonhole or blanket stitch into the appliqué with the tip of the needle returning to the edge. Continue in this manner all the way around the shape.

Cutting bias strips

For curved appliqué pattern pieces such as meandering vines, and for binding curved edges, you will need to cut strips on the bias of the fabric, that is diagonally across the grain of the fabric at 45^0 to the selvedge. Prepare a square or rectangle of the fabric and make sure the left edge is square. Place the ruler at 45^0 to the left edge and make a cut.

Then measure the width of the bias strip required and cut the first bias strip. Cut enough strips for the length required. Sew the strips together end to end with the seam at 45^0 to the edge of the bias strip.

Sew bias strips together end to end

Adding borders

Border strips have straight or mitred corners.

Straight corners

Lay out the quilt and measure it vertically through the centre. Cut two side strips this length. In *Quintessential Quilting*, the length of borders is given accurately but you may want to cut them with a little extra length, which can be adjusted once the quilt top is complete. Join the sides of the quilt top, matching the centres of both. Press. Lay out the quilt top again, and measure across the centre horizontally including the added borders. Cut the border strips to the required length and attach the strips to the top and bottom of the quilt top.

Adding borders with straight corners

Mitred corners

The length of the border required is the measurement of the quilt top plus twice the width of the border plus an extra 2in (5cm) to be on the safe side. Matching the centre of the border and the side of the quilt top, sew the borders to the four sides of the quilt top beginning and ending the seam ¼in (7.5mm) from the quilt top corners.

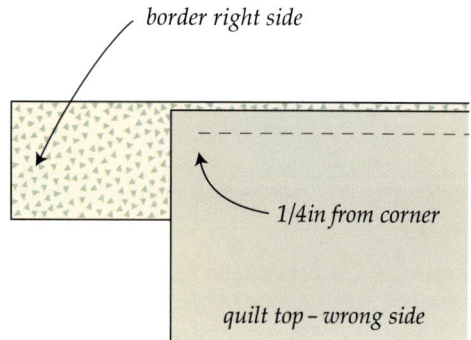

border right side

1/4in from corner

quilt top – wrong side

Step 1 When mitring corners, end the seam ¼in (7.5mm) from the quilt top corners.

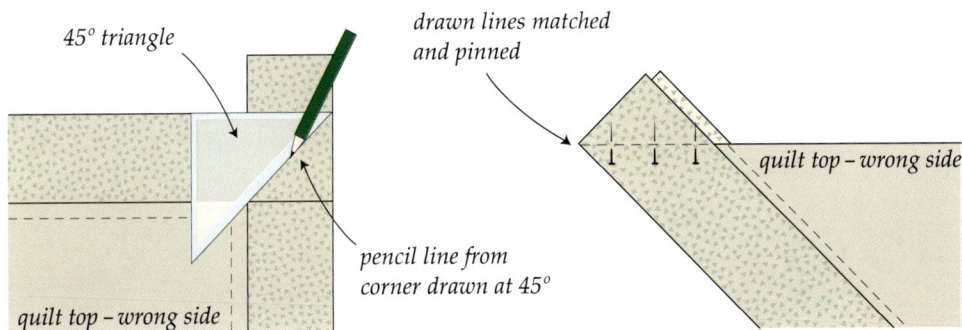

45° triangle

drawn lines matched and pinned

pencil line from corner drawn at 45°

quilt top – wrong side

quilt top – wrong side

Step 2 Press the seam allowance towards the border. Overlap the border strips at one corner and place a 90° right angle triangle along the raw edge of the top strip so its long edge intersects exactly where the seams meet in the corner. Draw along this edge with a pencil from the seam to the raw edge. Place the bottom border strip on top and repeat.

Step 3 Sew from the corner out to the raw edges. When you are happy that the corner seam is lying flat, trim the seam back to ¼in (7.5mm) and press open. Repeat with the other corners.

Finishing the quilt

Marking the quilt top

Press the completed quilt top one last time and trace the quilting design from the pattern sheet or a design of your choice onto the top using your preferred marker, already tested on a scrap of fabric. Most quilting lines are marked onto the fabric before it is sandwiched and pinned for quilting. Mark on a hard, flat surface and keep your marking tool sharp. A light under a glass-topped table will facilitate tracing.

Preparing the quilt sandwich

There is sufficient fabric in the materials listed in *Quintessential Quilting* for you to cut and piece the backing fabric 4in (10cm) larger than the quilt top. Once the backing is sewn, press all seams open. Secure a smoothed-out backing, right side down, to the floor or any other large surface with pins or masking tape, placed every 4in (10cm) around the edge. Add the batting – trimmed to just a little smaller than the backing and then the quilt top, right side up. Pin- or thread-baste the three layers together beginning at the centre. Baste around the edge of the quilt.

Quilt on the drawn lines or as desired. Quilting is simply a running stitch (by hand) or a line of stitching (by machine) which holds three layers together.

Adding a sleeve

To display the quilt on a wall or in an exhibition, it is advisable to add a sleeve to the back of the quilt before you bind the quilt.

Cut a strip of fabric before 6–8in (15–20cm) wide by the width of the quilt using a fabric the same as or blending with the backing fabric. Fold the ends under ½in (1.25cm) then again and stitch. Fold the strip in half lengthwise, wrong sides together. Align the raw edges with the top of the quilt back and baste in place.

This will be secured when the binding is sewn down. Blind stitch the bottom of the sleeve in place.

Examples of both machine and hand quilting

Quilt sleeve basted in place

Binding the quilt

In *Quintessential Quilting*, the binding is usually French-fold or doubled unless otherwise stated. Join the strips cut for the binding – usually 2½in (6.5cm) wide – into one continuous strip, sewing the strips together with a diagonal seam. Trim this seam to ¼in (7.5mm) and press open. Fold the binding in half, wrong sides together and press. Turn under the raw edges on one end of the binding strip. Trim the quilt top leaving ¼in (7.5mm) seam allowance. Trim the wadding and backing leaving ½in (1.5cm) seam allowance.

Begin at the centre of one side and align the raw edges of the binding with the raw edges of the quilt top. Sew through all layers, stopping ¼in (7.5mm) from the corner.

Backstitch and cut the threads. Remove the quilt from under the sewing machine foot. Fold the binding upwards and away from the quilt creating a diagonal fold.

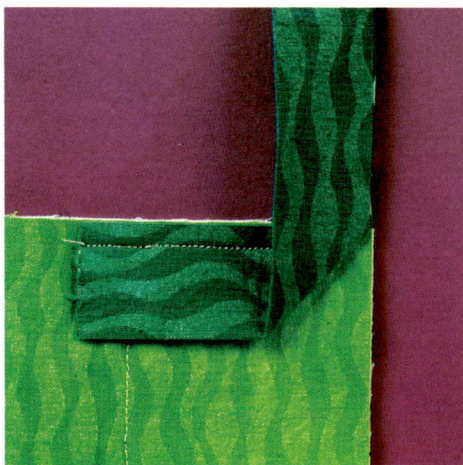

Fold binding up and away from quilt to create a diagonal fold

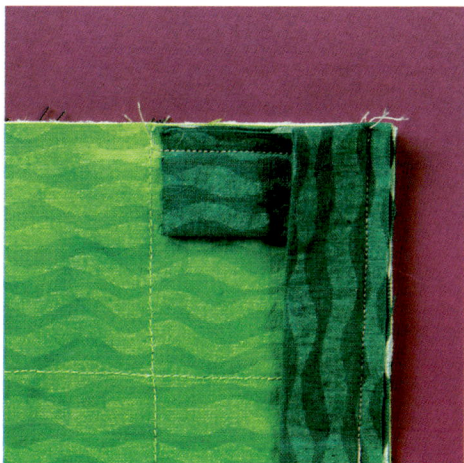

Start sewing again at the top of the quilt edge

Hold the fold in place and bring the binding in line with the next edge of the quilt. When you have reached the starting point, overlap the binding and slipstitch the ends together on the diagonal. Turn the binding to the back and slip stitch in place. At each corner, fold the binding to form mitres on both the front and the back of the quilt. Stitch these in place.

Banana lounge

MEGAN FISHER of Davidson, NSW, has created this brightly coloured quilt after being inspired by a quilt in the book *Razzle Dazzle Quilts* by well-known Australian quilt artist, Judy Hooworth. She adapted Judy's method for creating crazy pieced blocks, using some of her very favourite fabrics.

Materials

- Brightly coloured scraps to total about 2m (2¼yds) for the blocks

- 15cm (¼yd) dark blue fabric for inner border

- 1m (1⅛ yds) yellow fabric for outer border

- 40cm (½yd) hot pink fabric for binding

- 2.3m (2⅝ yds) backing fabric

- 125cm x 155cm (49in x 61in) batting

- Tissue paper – sufficient to cut 35 squares, 8in

- Rotary cutter and mat

- Pencil or water-erasable marking pen

- General sewing supplies

Finished Size: 45in x 57in

Note: Instructions are given in Imperial. The blocks are string pieced onto foundations. Megan used tissue paper for her foundations; tracing paper, freezer paper or thin typing paper is also suitable. Other possible foundations include interfacing or calico – however these will remain in the quilt, making it slightly heavier and a little harder to quilt by hand. Banana Lounge is in the private collection of Kirby Hocking, of Toorak, Victoria, and was made especially for her.

Diagram 1

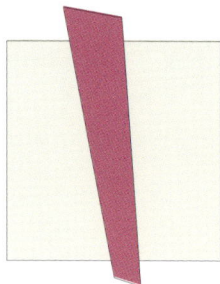
Diagram 2

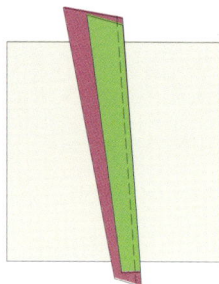
Diagram 3

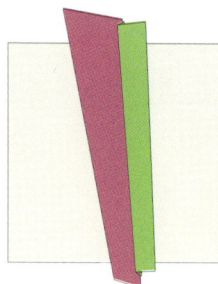
Diagram 4

Cut the fabric

From the scrap fabrics, cut:

 strips in widths that vary from 1in up to 3in wide.

Note: *The strips need to be about 8½ or 9in long – long enough to extend beyond the edges of the foundation square when placed at an angle across it. Cut at least half of the strips as wedge-shaped pieces – that is, pieces where the sides are not parallel and one end is wider than the other (see Diagram 1).*

From the dark blue fabric, cut:

 4 strips, 1in x width of fabric for the inner border.

From the yellow fabric, cut:

 5 strips, 7¼in x width of fabric for the outer border.

From the hot pink fabric, cut:

 6 strips, 2¼in x width of fabric for the binding. Join end to end.

From the backing fabric, cut:

 2 lengths, 125cm (47¼ in) x width of fabric. Remove the selvedges.

From the tissue or alternative foundation paper, cut:

 35 squares, 8in.

Make the blocks

1 Choose a strip of scrap fabric that is at least 8½in long. Place it right side up at an angle across the centre of a foundation square so that it extends at least ½in over each edge (see Diagram 2).

2 Choose a strip cut from a different scrap fabric and place it on top of the first strip, right sides together and matching right-hand raw edges (see Diagram 3).

3 Using a short stitch length, sew through the two fabric strips and the foundation using a ¼in seam allowance. Flip the second strip over so that it is right side up and press (see Diagram 4).

4 Continue adding strips of fabric on either side of the original strip until the entire foundation square is covered. Press after adding each strip. Trim the block to 6½in square. Repeat to make 35 string-pieced squares.

5 Gently tear the tissue paper off the back of the blocks. Handle the blocks carefully, as parts of the raw edges may not be on-grain.

Completed block

Assemble the quilt

1 Referring to the quilt photo, lay out the 35 blocks in 7 rows in a basket weave arrangement. In every second block the strips will run vertically and in the other blocks the strips will run horizontally. Play with the blocks until you find an arrangement of colours that you particularly like.

2 Join the blocks in rows of 5 blocks each, and then join the rows together.

Add the inner border

1 Measure the quilt top vertically through the centre. Join the 1in strips of dark blue fabric together to create one long strip. From it, cut two lengths equal to the vertical measurement for your quilt. Sew one of these to each side of the quilt.

2 Measure the quilt top horizontally through the centre. From the remaining dark blue strip, cut two strips this length. Sew one to the top and bottom of the quilt top.

Add the outer border

1 Measure the quilt top vertically through the centre. Join the strips of yellow fabric together to create one long strip. From it, cut two lengths equal to the vertical measurement of the quilt top. Sew one of these to the sides of the quilt.

2 Measure the quilt top horizontally through the centre. From the remaining yellow strip, cut two strips this length. Sew one to the top and bottom of the quilt.

Finish the quilt

1 Join the two pieces of backing fabric lengthwise. Trim to form the backing 49in x 61in.

2 Press the quilt top. Lightly trace a quilting pattern onto the top using a fine pencil or water-erasable marking pen if desired. Referring to 'Preparing the quilt sandwich' on page 28, layer the completed quilt top with batting and backing, and pin- or thread-baste the three layers together.

3 Quilt either by hand or machine. *Banana Lounge* was professionally quilted by Suzy Atkins of Quiltstuff Machine Quilting Services using an all-over pattern.

4 Add a hanging sleeve before binding if required (see adding a sleeve on page 29).

5 Referring to 'Binding the quilt' on page 30, bind the quilt using the hot pink fabric strip. Add a label. Enjoy your 'cure for the blues'!

Gone fishing

This is a fun way to make a quilt! Cathy Craig of Tea Tree, Tasmania made the quilt top in just two hours using wonderful hand-dyed fabrics. *Gone Fishing* was made as a gift for Cathy's father for his birthday in February 2002. He was delighted to hear the words, 'Yes Dad, you can take this one fishing!' (Cathy was introduced to the technique used in *Gone Fishing* by Lynette and Ruth for the Patchwork Angel, Queensland.)

Materials

- 12 fat quarters (FQs) [55cm x 50cm (21in x 18in)] hand-dyed fabric. This can be 12 different FQs or 2 FQs of 6 different fabrics.

- 50cm (⅝yd) fabric for binding

- 2.8m (3¼yds) backing fabric

- Piece of batting 170cm x 140cm (70in x 57in)

- Toning thread for sewing

- Sewing machine

- Rotary cutter, ruler and mat

- Iron

Finished Size: 164cm x 132cm (66in x 53in)

Note: No templates or quick cutting methods are required here as all cuts are made at the discretion of the quilter. Only guidelines are offered to achieve a good result with the technique. Cathy has quilted Gone Fishing *on her long arm quilting machine.*

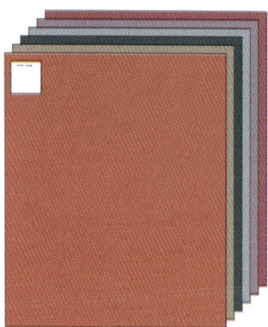

Diagram 1 – stack six numbered fat quarters

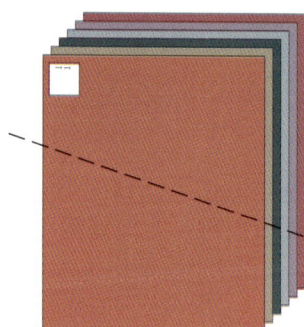

Diagram 2 – cut the stack

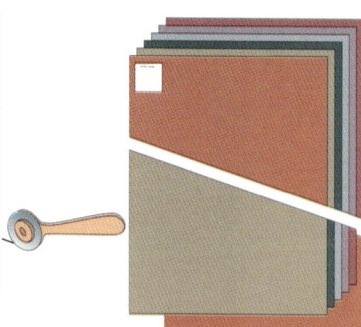

Diagram 3 – place the top piece on the bottom of the unnumbered stack

Make the blocks

Use 6 FQs at a time.

1 Pin a number 1 through 6 on six FQs in the upper left hand corner, then stack them into a pile (see Diagram 1).

Numbering the FQs is important as they need to be restacked in order after each cut and sew step. The numbering also ensures there is an even mix of fabrics in each block and that no two pieces of the same fabric end up side by side.

2 Make one cut through the stack. Just cut wherever you like (see Diagram 2).

Try to vary the placement of future cuts so as not to have a group of tiny pieces all in the centre of the block.

3 From the unnumbered stack of pieces, take the top piece and take it to the bottom of its stack (see Diagram 3).

Sew the top two pieces together, then the next two, on down the set. Press.

4 Restack the six-pieced FQs. Make sure the numbers in the upper left hand corner remain in order. Make cut #2 (see Diagram 4).

5 Take two pieces from the top of the unnumbered stack and take them to the bottom as before. Sew the block back together again and press. Restack, always keeping the numbered pieces in numerical order, 1 through 6, in the upper left hand corner.

6 Make cut #3. Take three pieces from the unnumbered stack to the bottom and sew the block back together again. Restack as before.

7 Make cut #4. Take four pieces from the unnumbered stack to the bottom. Sew the block back together and restack as before.

8 Make cut #5. Take five pieces from the unnumbered stack to the bottom. Sew the block back together and restack as before.

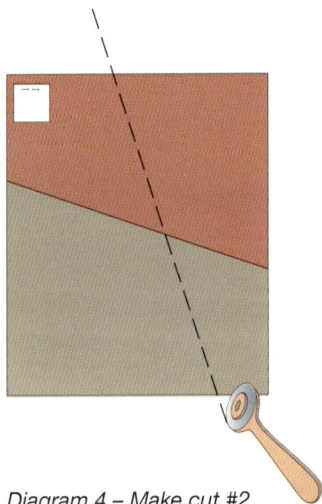

Diagram 4 – Make cut #2

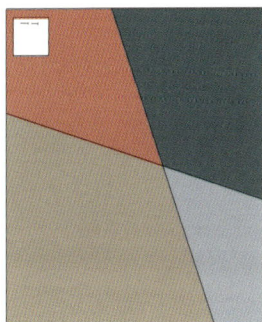

Diagram 5 – Place the two top pieces on the bottom and sew the block together again

9 Make cut #6, take three pieces from the unnumbered stack to the bottom. Before resewing the block together for the last time, go through the blocks to see if you are happy with the fabric mixes. If not, simply move the pieces until your are happy with the combination. Sew the block back together and restack as before. Trim each block to 17in x 19in.

10 Make the next 6 blocks using the remaining 6 FQs.

Assemble the quilt top

1 Sew the blocks together in 3 rows of 4 blocks. Press the seams of alternate rows in the opposite direction.

2 Sew the rows together, referring to the quilt photo.

Finish the quilt

1 Cut the piece of backing fabric in half lengthwise. Remove the selvedges, then sew the two pieces together lengthwise. Trim the backing to 170cm x 140cm (70in x 57in).

2 Sandwich the quilt, referring to 'Preparing the quilt sandwich' on page 28 and baste.

3 Quilt as desired. This quilt was professionally quilted by Cathy Craig of Needles and Pins Quilting, Tasmania, using a freehand swirl pattern, adding to the movement of the colours in the quilt provided by fabrics from the *Dyed and Gone to Heaven* range by Lisa Walton, Sydney NSW.

4 Cut 6 strips of binding fabric, 6.5cm (2½in) x width of fabric. Join the strips end to end into one long strip. Referring to page 30, bind the quilt. Add a label.

The red centre

Eastwood Patchwork Quilters chose crazy patchwork for *The Red Centre*, their donation to the QUILTS 2000 project, because it is quick and easy to make, whether by hand or machine. Make this cosy quilt from Australian wool in a jiffy, and tie it so that it's ready to take centre stage at your next picnic. A great weekend project!

Materials

- Woollen fabric comes in various widths. Measurements are given here for fabric 110cm (42in) wide.

- 30cm red wool fabric for centres

- Assorted wool fabric scraps equivalent to 2.5m. Include plaids, checks and plains

- 2.2m cream homespun or equivalent for the foundation fabric

- 1.8m plaid wool for border

- 3m backing fabric

- Black Perle embroidery thread for tying

- Crewel needle

Finished Size: 52in x 68in (130cm x 170cm)
Block Size: 8½in (21.5cm)

Note: Instructions are given in Imperial and Metric measurements.

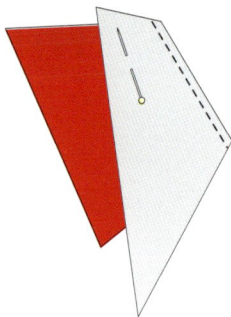

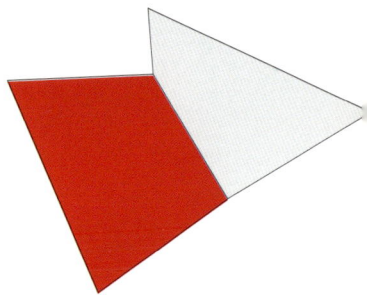

Diagram 1   *Diagram 2*   *Diagram 3*

Cut the fabric

From the homespun, cut:

   35 squares, 9in x 9in (23cm x 23cm).

From the red wool, cut:

   35 irregular 4- or 5-sided shapes (refer to
   the photograph of the quilt for examples).

From the assorted wool scraps, cut:

   approximately 350 irregular shaped pieces
   for the crazy patchwork.

From the plaid wool, cut:

   2 strips, 6½in x 401/2in (16.5cm x
   101.5cm) for short borders.
   2 strips, 6½in x 68½in (16.5cm x 171.5cm)
   for long borders.

From the backing fabric, cut:

   2 sections, 36in x 56in (90cm x 140cm).
   Join lengthwise to form the backing 72in x
   56in (180cm x 140cm).

Assemble the block

1 Place one of the red wool shapes right side
up in the centre of a homespun foundation
square. Pin it in place (see Diagram 1).

2 Select a second patch from a different
fabric and place it right side down on
top of the red centre. Make sure one of the
sides is parallel to one of the edges of the red
centre. Pin this shape in place, then sew a
¼in (7.5mm) seam allowance by hand or
machine (see Diagram 2).

3 Fold out the second shape and press.
Trim the excess fabric if necessary (see
Diagram 3).

4 Add a third shape by lying it right side
down over the red centre and the second
patch. Pin and stitch in place as before (see
Diagram 4).

Fold the third shape over and press (see
Diagram 5). Trim as required.

5 Continue adding shapes until the
foundation square is covered (see
Diagram 6). Trim the block to an 8½in (21.5cm)
square (see Diagram 7). Make 35 blocks.

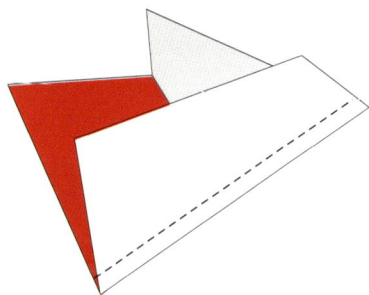

Diagram 4

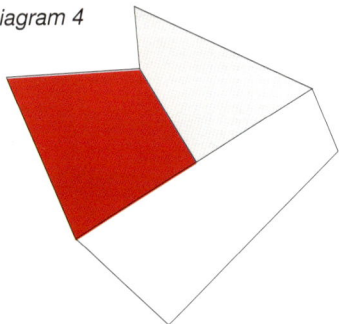

Diagram 5

Diagram 6

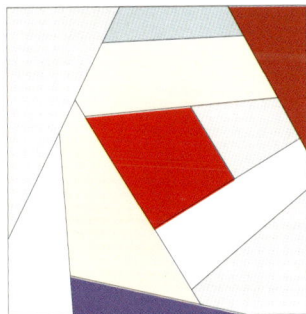

Diagram 7

Assemble the quilt top

1 Join the blocks in seven rows of five blocks per row. Join the rows of blocks.

2 Referring to 'Adding borders on page 26, add the plaid borders.

Finish the quilt

1 Place the quilt top onto the centre of the backing fabric, right sides together. Pin in place, then trim the backing to the same size as the quilt top. Sew around the edges of the quilt top and the backing, leaving a small opening for turning. Turn the quilt through this opening, then close the opening with a slip stitch.

2 Lay the quilt on the floor or on a large table ready for tying. Decide where you want to tie the quilt and mark each position with a pin. For *The Red Centre*, each block is tied through the centre red patch at each corner and the middle of each side. The borders are tied along the middle every 4in (7.5cm).

3 Thread a crewel needle with 30in (75cm) Perle embroidery thread or another strong thread. Begin with a ¼in (7.5mm) stitch at the first pin, pulling the thread through the layers of the quilt until there is a 3in (7.5cm) tail. Leave the needle threaded and tie the ends securely using a square or reef knot. Cut the ends to the length desired.

4 Label the quilt.

Butterflies in bloom

Jenny Thurling of Patchwork Mania, Camden, NSW, loves every range of fabric in her shop, particularly the reproduction '30s feed sack prints. Choosing her favourites from this collection, she has created *Butterflies in Bloom*. The quilt is quick and easy to make on the machine and sure to delight all those who have collections of '30s fabrics and love making scrappy quilts.

Materials

- 10cm (1/8yd) black background floral for the flower centres

- 3m (3 3/8yds) white homespun for the blocks

- 18 different floral fat quarters (50cm x 55cm [20in x 22in])

- Scraps of green fabrics for the stems

- Scrap of black fabric for the butterfly bodies

- 1m (1 1/8yds) mauve fabric for Border 1 and binding

- 1m (1 1/8yds) double-sided fusible web

- Machine embroidery thread to match the appliqué, stranded embroidery thread if appliquéing by hand

- Batting at least 162cm x 188cm (64in x 82in) 4m (4 1/2yds) backing fabric

Finished size: 152cm x 178cm (60in x 78in)
Block Size: 9in

Note: *Instructions are given in Imperial measurements for quick cutting and piercing*

Cut the fabric

From the white homespun, cut:

18 squares, 10½in for the blocks with appliqué. Cut these back to 9½in after appliqué.

12 strips, 3½in x width of fabric. Cross cut into 140 squares, 3½in for the Nine-patch blocks and the pieced border.

From each floral fabric, cut:

4 squares, 3½in for the flower blocks, a total of 72 squares

5 squares, 3½in for the Nine-patch blocks. You will need 17 sets of 5 squares.

1 square, 4½in for the flowers

From the floral fabrics, cut:

88 squares, 3½in. Use a good mixture of all fabrics.

From the mauve border fabric, cut:

7 strips, 2in x width of fabric for Border 1

9 strips, 2½in x width of fabric for the binding. Join end to end.

Prepare the appliqué

1 Using the patterns on page 49, trace onto the smooth side of the fusible web 18 flowers, 18 flower centres, 18 stems and 4 butterfly bodies, 4 large left wings, 4 small left wings, 4 large right wings and 4 small right wings.

2 Cut out roughly about ¼in outside the traced line and iron onto the wrong side of the fabrics selected for the appliqué.

3 Cut out all pieces neatly on the line. Set the butterfly pieces aside.

4 Peel the backing off the fusible web, position the flowers, flower centres and stems on the white homespun squares using the quilt photo as a guide. Press in place. Do not drag the iron.

5 Buttonhole stitch around each shape, then centring the flowers, trim the blocks back to 9½in once all the appliqué stitching is completed.

Make the flower blocks

1 Draw a diagonal line on the wrong side of each of the seventy two 3½in floral squares cut for the flower blocks.

2 Place one square in each corner of the trimmed 9½in white homespun blocks and sew on the line.

3 Trim the corners, leaving the homespun square underneath intact, then fold out the floral triangle and press firmly taking care not to distort the square (see Diagram 1).

Make the nine-patch blocks

Sew 5 floral and 4 white 3½in squares as shown in Diagram 2. Make 18 blocks.

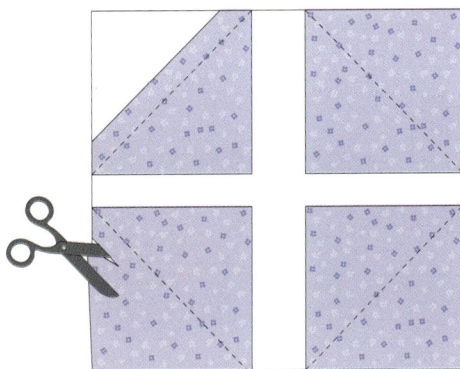

Diagram 1

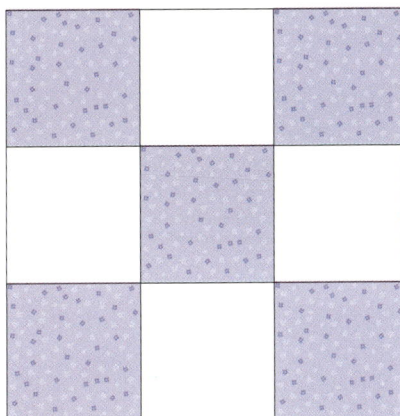

Diagram 2

Assemble the quilt

1 Lay out the Nine-patch blocks and the floral appliqué blocks as shown in the quilt photo. Sew the blocks together in rows, then sew the rows together.

2 Join the seven 2in strips of mauve fabric for Border 1 into one long length. Measure across the quilt centre and cut two pieces from the strip to that length. Sew them to the top and bottom of the quilt. Measure the length through the middle of the quilt top and cut two pieces from the strip to that length. Sew the mauve strips to the sides of the quilt. Press the seams towards the border.

3 From the assortment of white and floral 3½in squares, sew pairs of one floral and one white square. Make 15 pairs for the top and bottom Border 2 and 21 pairs for each side Border 2. Sew the pairs together to form a checkerboard as shown in the quilt photo.

4 To each end of the checkerboard panel, sew a 6½in strip of the mauve Border 1 fabric.

5 Make 4 four-patch blocks using only floral fabrics. Sew these to each end of the two side Border 2 checkerboard panels.

6 Add the shorter top and bottom Border 2 panels to the quilt centre. Then sew the longer panels to the sides of the quilt top.

7 Appliqué a butterfly in each corner, referring to the quilt photo for placement. Embroider the antennae.

Finish the quilt

1 Cut the backing fabric into two lengths, remove the selvedges and sew together lengthwise. Trim to 64in x 82in.

2 Referring to 'Preparing the quilt sandwich', on page 28, sandwich the backing, batting and quilt top. Pin or thread baste.

3 Quilt as desired. Jenny has stippled around each flower and quilted in the ditch for the nine-patch blocks and the checkerboard border.

4 Bind the quilt using the long strip of 2½in mauve fabric and referring to 'Binding the quilt' on page 30.

5 Label your quilt and enjoy!

Flower Template

Cut 18 of each of the flower stem, flower centre and flower. Image has been reversed for tracing onto double-sided, fusible web.

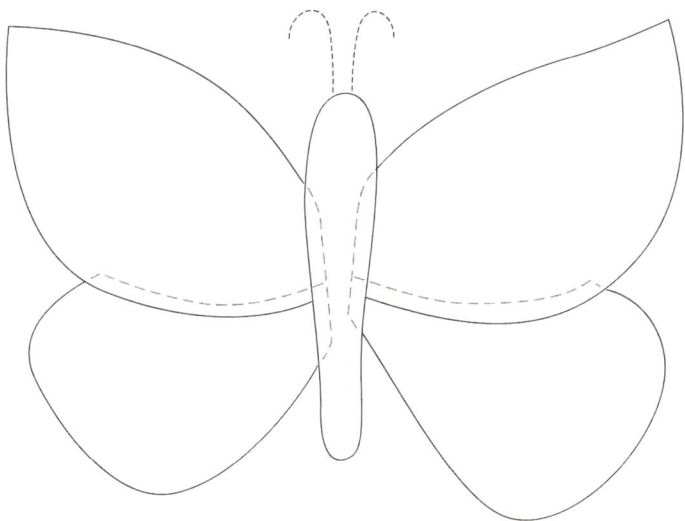

Butterfly Template

Cut 4 of each of the small and large left and right wings and 4 butterfly bodies. Image has been reversed for tracing onto double-sided fusible web.

Blue grotto

Designing quilts comes naturally to Anne Bartlett from Launceston, Tasmania, who originally presented the design for *Blue Grotto* as a Mystery Quilt for the members of the Tasmanian Quilters. Anne has provided all the instructions for her stunning quilt here, so you don't have to go through the agony of not knowing what the finished quilt will look like.

Materials

- 2.75m (3yds) assorted cream print fabrics

- 3m (3⅜ yds) assorted blue print fabric scraps (include some purples and greens)

- 3.5m (3⅞ yds) assorted black print fabrics (include a few dark grey prints)

- 40cm (½yd) gold print fabric for the centre medallion and Border 5

- 40cm (½yd) black/gold print fabric for Border 3

- 50cm (⅝ yd) blue/purple print fabric for Border 2

- 60cm (¾yd) cream fabric for binding

- 5.9m (6½yds) backing fabric

- Batting to measure 230cm x 230cm (90in x 90in)

Finished Size: 84in x 84in

Note: Instructions are given in Imperial measurements for template free cutting. For the quilt layout diagram, see page 62.

Cut the fabric

From the assorted cream fabrics, cut:

4 strips, 3in x width of fabric. Cross cut into 44 squares, 3in for the centre star and the centre medallion.

13 strips, 3½in x width of fabric. Cross cut into 136 squares, 3½in for the Ohio Star blocks and Border 8.

4 squares, 3⅞in for Border 1 and 2

8 strips, 4¼in x width of fabric. Cross cut into 66 squares, 4¼in for Border 1 and the Ohio Star blocks.

2 strips, 7¼in x width of fabric. Cross cut into 6 squares, 7¼in for Border 2.

1 strip, 5½in x width of fabric. Cross cut into 8 rectangles, 5½in x 3in for the centre medallion.

2 squares, 16in from the same fabric. Cut each square along one diagonal to give 4 setting triangles for the centre medallion.

From the assorted blue fabrics, cut:

1 square, 5½in for the centre star

2 strips, 5½in x width of fabric. Cross cut into 16 rectangles, 5½in x 3in for the Flying Geese units for the centre medallion.

2 squares, 3⅜in for the centre medallion

19 strips, 3½in x width of fabric. Cross cut into 200 squares, 3½in for Border 7 and 8.

3 strips, 3⅞in x width of fabric. Cross cut into 26 squares, 3⅞in for the centre medallion and Borders 1, 2 & 7

4 strips, 4¼in x width of fabric. Cross cut into 30 squares, 4¼in. (2 for bias squares for Border 1, 28 for the Ohio Stars.)

2 strips, 7¼in x width of fabric. Cross cut into 6 squares, 7¼in for Border 2.

From the assorted black fabrics cut:

4 strips, 3in x width of fabric. Cross cut into 48 squares, 3in for the centre star and the centre medallion.

2 squares 3⅜in for the centre medallion

11 strips, 3½in x width of fabric. Cross cut into 112 squares, 3½in for the Ohio Star blocks in Border 6.

2 squares, 3⅞in for Border 7

5 strips, 4¼in x width of fabric. Cross cut into 38 squares, 4¼in for Border 1 and the Ohio Star blocks.

17 strips, 3½in x width of fabric. Cross cut into 100 rectangles, 6½in x 3½in for Border 7 and Border 8.

From gold fabric for the centre medallion and Border 4, cut:

9 strips, 1½in x width of fabric

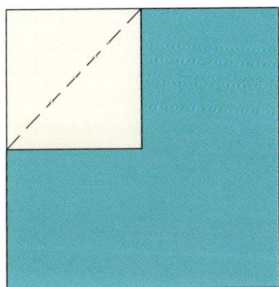

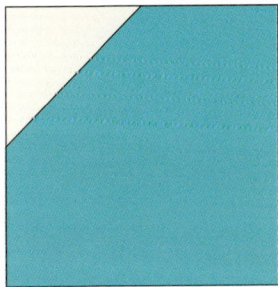

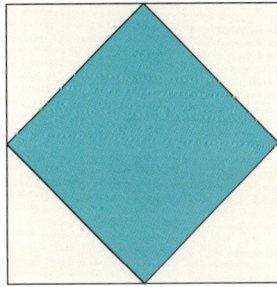

Diagram 1 – square in a square

Diagram 2 – the centre star block

From black/gold fabric for Border 4, cut:

    5 strips, 2½in x width of fabric

From blue/purple fabric print for Border 4, cut:

    5 strips, 3½in x width of fabric

From the binding fabric, cut:

    9 strips, 2½in x width of fabric. Join end
    to end.

Make the centre star

1 Draw a diagonal line on the wrong side of four 3in cream squares. Place a cream square in the corner of the 5½in blue square and sew along the diagonal line. Trim the cream fabric triangle closest to one corner leaving ¼in allowance. Fold back triangle and press. Repeat on the remaining three corners to make a square in a square (see Diagram 1).

2 Make 16 Flying Geese units using 32 cream 3in squares and 16 blue 5½in x 3in rectangles. Using these Flying Geese units and 32 black 3in squares, make 16 Unit A (see Helpful Hint).

3 Sew 2 Unit A to opposite sides of the square in a square unit. Sew a cream 3in square to each end of 2 Unit A. Sew them to the remaining two sides of the square in a square unit. The star block formed should measure 10½in square (See Diagram 2). The remaining 12 Unit As will be used to complete the centre medallion.

Helpful Hint

Making Unit A

Take one Flying Geese Unit and two 3in squares of black print fabric for each Unit A.

1 Draw a diagonal line from corner to corner on the wrong side of the black square. Draw a second diagonal line 1/2in away from the first. With right sides together place a square on one end of the Flying Geese unit. Sew along both of the marked diagonal lines.

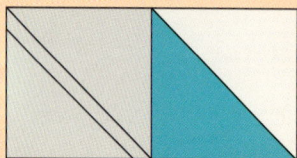

2 Cut midway between the two seam lines and press open. Save discarded bias squares for another project.

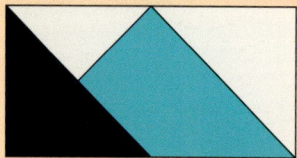

3 Repeat steps 1–2 with the second square on the opposite end of the Flying Geese unit.

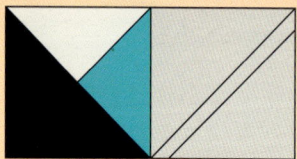

4 Press open. Finished unit will measure the same size as the Flying Geese unit.

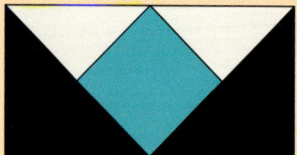

Unit A

Making bias squares using two squares

1 Draw a diagonal from corner to corner on the wrong side of the lighter of the two squares. With right sides together, place the lighter square on top of the darker square and sew ¼in either side of the diagonal.

2 Cut along the diagonal.

3 Press open with the seam allowance to the darker fabric.

Step 1

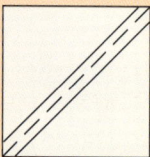

Step 2

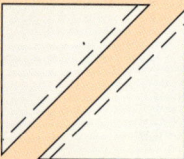

Step 3

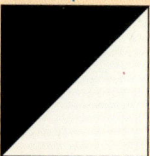

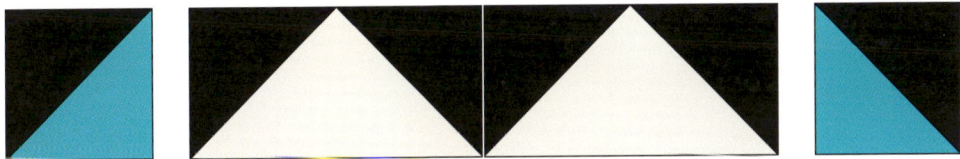

Diagram 3

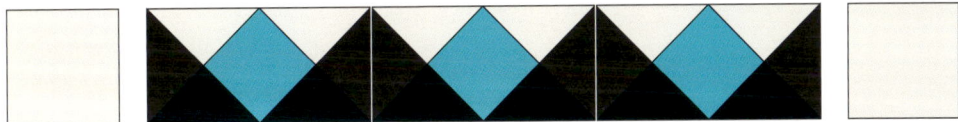

Diagram 4

Assemble the centre medallion

1 Make 8 Flying Geese units using 8 cream 5½in x 3in rectangles and 16 black 3in squares. Make 4 blue/black bias squares from 2 blue and 2 black 3⅜in squares.

2 Sew the Flying Geese units into 4 strips of 2. Sew 2 strips to opposite sides of the star block. Sew a blue/black bias square to each end of remaining strips (see Diagram 3), then sew these strips to the remaining sides of the star block. The centre should now measure 16½in square.

3 Sew the remaining 12 Unit As into 4 strips of 3. Sew two strips to opposite sides of the centre. Sew a cream 3in square to each of the remaining strips (see Diagram 4) then sew these strips to the remaining two sides of the centre. The centre should now measure 21½in square.

4 Sew 2 cream setting triangles to opposite sides of the centre block. Press seam allowance towards the cream triangles. Sew the remaining 2 cream setting triangles to the other sides of the centre block. Trim the centre medallion for the quilt top to 28½in square (see Diagram 5).

Diagram 5 – centre medallion of quilt top

5 From the 1½in gold strips, cut 2 strips, 28½in and 2 strips, 30½in. Sew the 28½in strips to opposite sides of the medallion centre, then sew the 30½in strips to the top and bottom of the medallion. The quilt centre should measure 30½in square.

Add border 1

1 Make 20 cream/black bias squares using 10 cream and 10 black 4¼in squares.

2 Draw a diagonal on the wrong side of 20 blue 3⅞in squares. With right sides together, place a blue square on top of a cream/black bias square so the diagonal runs from point A to point B (see Diagram 6).

3 Sew ¼in either side of the diagonal then cut along the diagonal. Press the seam allowance towards the blue fabric. Make 20 Unit B and 20 Unit B reversed (see Diagram 7).

4 Make 4 cream/blue bias squares using 2 cream and 2 blue 3⅞in squares.

5 Sew the Unit Bs into 4 strips of 5 units and sew the Unit Brs into 4 strips of 5 units. Sew each strip of Unit B to a strip of Unit Br to form the strips for Border 1 (see Diagram 8). Sew two Border 1 strips to each side of the quilt centre. Sew a cream/blue bias square to each end of remaining Border 1 strips (see Diagram 8) then sew to the top and bottom of the quilt centre. The quilt top should now measure 36½in.

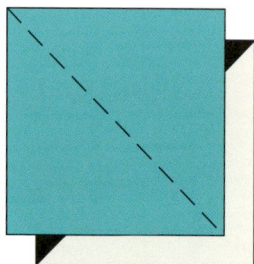

Diagram 6 – Making Unit B

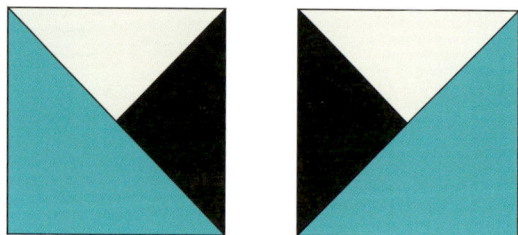

Diagram 7 – Unit B and Unit Br

Diagram 8 – Border 1 with bias squares

Diagram 9 – Border 2 strip

Diagram 10 – Border 2 strip sewn with a partial seam

Add border 2

1 Cut 6 cream and 6 blue 7¼in squares diagonally twice to give 24 cream and 24 blue quarter-square triangles. Cut 2 cream and 2 blue 3⅞in squares along one diagonal to give 4 cream and 4 blue half-square triangles.

2 Join the triangles together to form four strips (see Diagram 9). Each strip will consist of six cream and six blue triangles with a cream triangle at one end and a blue triangle at the other end.

3 Sew a strip to one side of quilt top (see Diagram 10). The strip is longer than the width of the quilt top so sew only a partial seam.

4 Sew the second strip to the side adjacent to the first, the third strip to the side adjacent to the second and the fourth to the remaining side. Finish sewing the seam on the first side only after the fourth Border 2 strip has been added. The quilt top should now measure 42½in square.

Add borders 3, 4 and 5

1 Join the 5 strips of black/gold print, 2½in wide, together to form one long strip. From this strip cut 2 strips, 42½in long and 2 strips 46½in long. Sew the short strips to either side of the quilt top, then sew the long strips to the top and bottom of the quilt top to complete Border 3. The quilt top should now measure 46½in square.

2 Join the 5 strips of blue/purple print, 3½in wide, together to form one long strip. From this strip, cut 2 strips 46½in long and 2 strips 52½in long. Sew the short strips to either side of quilt top, then sew the long strips to the top and bottom of the quilt top to complete Border 4. The quilt top should now measure 52½in square.

3 Join five strips of gold fabric, 1½in wide, together to form one long strip. From this strip cut two strips 52½in long and two strips 54½in long. Sew the short strips to either side of the quilt top, then sew the long strips to the top and bottom of the quilt top to compete Border 5. The quilt top should now measure 54½in square.

Add border 6 – Ohio Stars

1 To make the hourglass sections of the Ohio Star blocks, make 56 cream/blue bias squares using 28 cream and 28 blue 4¼in squares and make 56 cream/black bias squares using 28 cream and 28 black 4¼in squares.

2 Draw one diagonal on the wrong side of the cream/blue squares from point W to point Z across the seam. With right sides together place cream/blue squares on cream/black squares so that points A and X, B and W, C and Z and D and Y are aligned.

3 Sew ¼in either side of the drawn diagonal, then cut along the diagonal line. Press open to make 112 hourglass units.

Diagram 11 – the Ohio Star block for Border 6

4 Referring to Diagram 11, assemble the Ohio Star blocks. Sew 2 hourglass blocks to opposite sides of a cream 3½in square making sure a blue triangle is joined to the cream square. Sew a black 3½in square to each side of 2 hourglass blocks so that a cream triangle is joined to the black squares. Sew rows together to form an Ohio Star block. Make 28. The finished block should measure 9½in square.

5 Sew 6 Ohio Star blocks together to make a Border 6 strip. Make 2. Join these to either side of the quilt top.

6 Sew 8 Ohio Star blocks together to form a strip. Make 2. Sew these border strips to the top and bottom of the quilt top. The quilt top should now measure 72½in square.

Diagram 12 – making hourglass blocks

Diagram 13 – Border 7

Add border 7

1 Make 48 Flying Geese using the black 6½in x 3½in rectangles and 96 blue 3½in squares.

2 Make 4 blue/black bias squares using two blue and two black 3⁷⁄₈in squares.

3 Sew the Flying Geese into 4 strips of 12 (see Diagram 13). Sew 2 strips to either side of the quilt top. Sew a blue/black bias square to each end of the remaining 2 strips then sew them to the top and bottom of the quilt top. The quilt top should now measure 78½in square.

Add border 8

1 Make 52 Flying Geese using the black 6½in x 3½in rectangles and 104 blue 3½in squares. Using these Flying Geese units and 104 cream 3½in squares, make 52 Unit A (see Helpful Hint, page 54).

2 Sew 4 strips of 13 Unit A. Sew two Unit A strips either side of the quilt top. Sew a cream 3½in square to each end of the remaining 2 Unit A strips then sew to the top and bottom of the quilt top. The finished top measures 84½in square.

Finish the quilt

1 Cut two lengths 92in (235cm) of backing fabric and remove the selvedge. Cut the remaining backing through the centre, remove the selvedge and join to give a backing piece 92in x 22in (235cm x 55cm) trimmed. Sew the three pieces together to form the backing. Trim to 92in x 92in (235cm x 235cm).

2 Referring to 'Preparing the quilt sandwich' on page 28, layer the backing, batting and completed quilt top. Pin- or thread- baste the three layers together.

3 Quilt as desired. *Blue Grotto* was quilted by Cathy Craig, of Needles & Pins Quilting, using a continuous line pattern.

4 Trim the edge of the quilt. Add a sleeve before binding if the quilt is going to be displayed. (See 'Adding a sleeve' on page 29).

5 Bind the quilt, referring to page 30.

6 Make and sew label on to back of quilt. Enjoy!

Quilt layout diagram

Stitchery

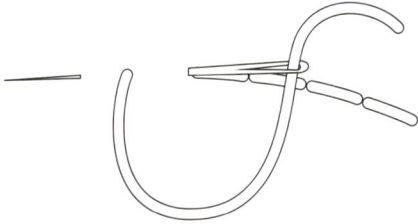

Backstitch

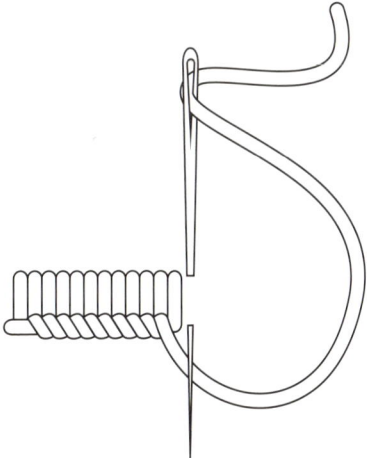

Buttonhole stitch

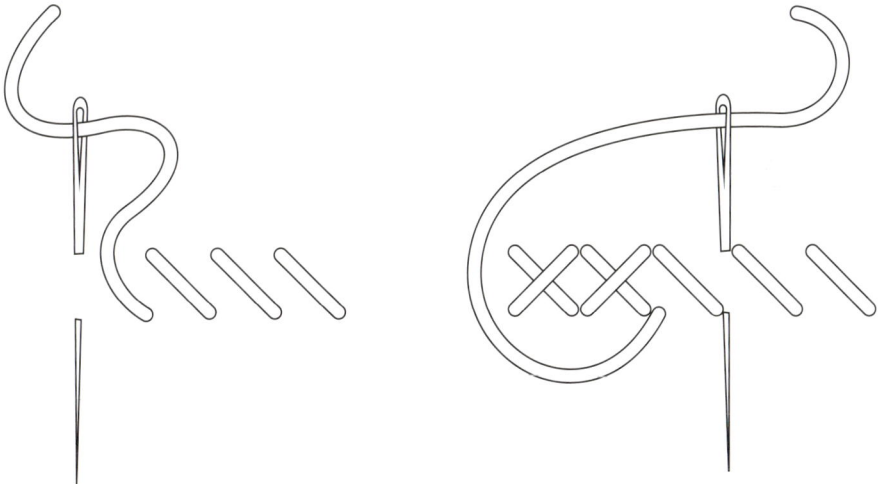

Cross-stitch

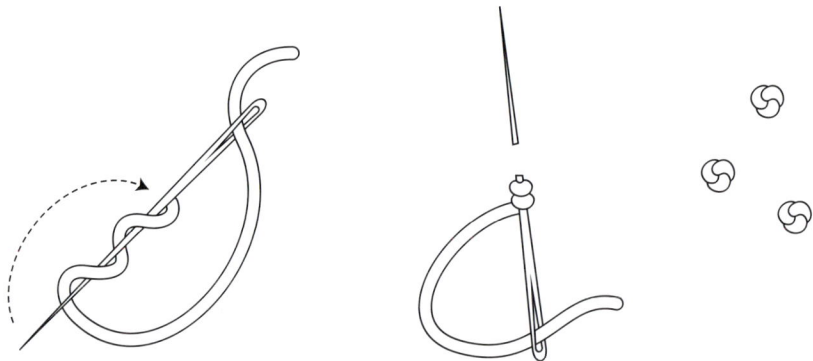

French knot

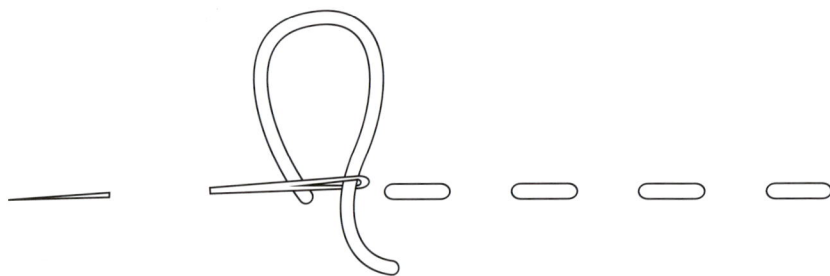

Running stitch

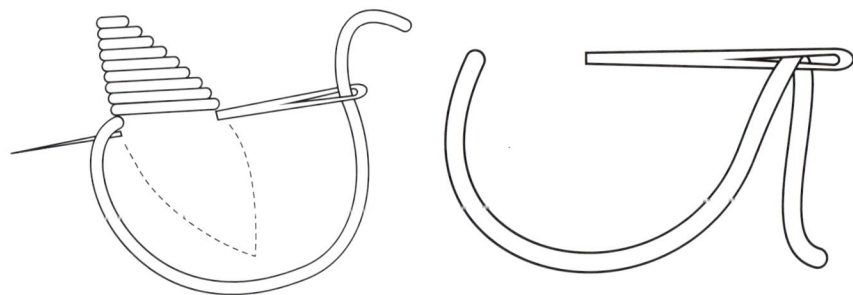

Satin stitch

Straight stitch